# MICHELLE DENNIS EVANS

Sink, Drift, or Swim

Copyright © 2025 Michelle Dennis Evans

Published by Armour Books
PO Box 492, Corinda QLD 4075
Australia

ISBN: 978-1-925380-97-2 (paperback)

Unless otherwise indicated, Scripture quotations are taken from THE HOLY BIBLE, NEW INTERNATIONAL VERSION®, NIV® Copyright © 1973, 1978, 1984, 2011 by Biblica, Inc.® Used by permission. All rights reserved worldwide.

A catalogue record for this book is available from the National Library of Australia

Creator: Evans, Michelle D., author.
Title: Sink, drift, or swim / Michelle Dennis Evans.
ISBN: 9781922135377 (paperback)
Target Audience: For young adults.
Subjects: Families--Fiction.
Fathers and daughters--Fiction.
Fishing--Fiction.
Suspense fiction.
Young adult fiction.
Bildungsromans.

This is a work of fiction. Names, characters, businesses, places, events and incidents are either the products of the author's imagination or used in a fictitious m anner. A ny r esemblance t o a ctual persons, living or dead, or actual events is purely coincidental.

All rights reserved. No part of this publication may be reproduced, stored in, or introduced into a retrieval system, or transmitted, in any form, or by any means—electronic, mechanical, photocopying, recording or otherwise—except for brief quotations for printed reviews, without the prior written permission of the publisher.

Cover Design: TLC Graphics, USA

# Dedicated To

Shane, Jacob, Tiara, Rita-Lily and Louella.
Your love keeps me afloat.

# Coffee

A hint of spring
whispers in my ears
that dreams can come true
and childhood friends
could possibly evolve into something ...

I shake off the thought
and kick my feet up
onto the floral outdoor lounge.
Hug my coffee mug.
School is out
for a couple of weeks.

Rest.
Breathe.
Study later.

A gust of wind
flicks a waft of fresh cut grass
through the air.
Rest?
Yeah, right!

Coffee to drink,
people to see,
days to fill.

I smile as
a wagtail sings to me.
The rattle of our screen door
grabs my attention
as footsteps punctuate the air.

# The Invitation

'Rina,' Dad calls.
Like everyone else
in this sleepy town
he dropped the Vale
from Valerina
years ago.

I can't recall a time
he ever called me by
my full name—
except in that song
he used to sing.

'I've got the boat this weekend.
I can't take everyone.
What do you say?
It's been a while since just
you and I hung out.'

It could be worse.
He could have asked me to grab a gun
and head west to hunt.
His other favourite pastime.
Second only to fishing offshore.

But it was the boat
on offer.
Likely to take up half a day.
What should I say?

# Not Alone

Others will be there too.
Not just Dad and me.
Dad's best mate Johnno,
Johnno's son Jayden,
Johnno's brother Al,
and Al's boy Kai.

As Dad ran through the list
it was glaringly apparent
I would be the only girl
on a boat filled with men fishing
and boys who'd rather ride skateboards.
Boys who'd prefer one of my brothers
to be on the boat—
not me.

No matter what,
the boat would be full.
It's the way it goes.
Word gets out.
The boat's about to float.
Blokes like my dad
rarely head out alone.
There's always a tribe
ready to drop everything
and jump on board.

# Brothers

I have two brothers
who'd both love to go.
But no,
Dad has asked me,
and I have to make the decision;
a decision that will leave
one brother asking, "Why not me?"
and the other will just ask, "Why?"

But I know those questions
never sway Dad.
It's a thing he has
about spending time with each of us
in situations where
we aren't completely comfortable.
And so I've learnt not to question.
But it doesn't stop me
wondering why.

# Asked

I find Mum in her room
folding washing.
Her legs up
on a stool
as she hums
to tunes
playing on the radio.

'Dad asked me to go—'

'On the boat?'
She finishes my sentence
with a hint of question,
a common trait of hers.
'Are you going to go?'

'What do you think?'
I raise my eyebrows
as I glance towards
her swollen ankles.
'Will you be okay?'

'Of course I will.
You'll only be gone a few hours.
You know how Dad loves to catch up,
one on one,
from time to time.'

I nod.
I knew
he did his best
to get round to a date
with each of us.
Even surrounded by others,
he'll find a moment
to get personal,

dig deeper,
try and get me to divulge
my deepest secrets.

'Yes, go.'
Mum groaned and rubbed
her protruding belly.
'We'll be fine.'

# A Local Café

I head out for a walk,
think over my answer.
Dad needs to know.
He's the orderly type,
plans in advance.
Prepares way before time.
Ticks all the boxes.

I know
he'd want to make sure
he has the lifejacket
in the right colour
and the right size.
And he would be making plans
to have food for my disease.

It seems like such an effort.
So much planning,
for just a couple of hours.

Fishing isn't
in my top ten.
It would be lucky to make
my top one hundred.

Dad is my only.
The one and only dad
in my life.

Didn't he know I'd be happy
with something as simple as
sitting and sipping a hot drink,
and nibbling a treat
at our local café?

# Bittersweet

My feet fall flat.
Indecision clings.

Waves.
Deep water filled with sharks.

My stomach churns
at the thought.
How will I cope?

The sun returns
from its brief interlude.
I look up and watch a cloud
head south.
Sunrays hit my eyes.
A dozen sneezes
splutter from my mouth.
And then
another round begins.

I need shade
to stop the sneeze.
I dash around the corner
into our local café
and pull a napkin from the dispenser.
Turning away from the counter
I blow my nose.

'Would you like to order?' he asks
in his luscious voice
that ripples through the air.

I throw the napkin
into the bin.

'Latte,' I respond,
hoping to connect
with him
in the moment
if I
        pause
a little longer ...
        Maybe?

'Another already?'
He blinks.
'Second for the day, hey?'
The breeze from his lashes
warms my mouth to a smile.

I nod.
Plus the two I had at home ...
Yep, coffee is my crutch.

He grabs a paper cup,
his lips slightly parted
like an invitation to a kiss.
I grab the counter.
My fingers curl.
My toes splay.
Before I can stop myself
        I lean forward ...
then wonder if he's noticed.
I lean back
and hope he didn't.

He pushes the lid on the cup
and exchanges it for money.

I take a sip as our eyes
                lock.

His brown.
Mine blue.
I search for his soul
through his chocolate caverns.
Until he blinks another breeze
and the moment is gone.

'Thanks,' I say.

'You're welcome.
See you again soon.'
His words sing a melody
in my ears like no other.
I turn
and take another sip.
Coffee
A bitter welcome on my tongue.
I swallow
My heartbeat quickens
at the thought
of that sweet soul.

Of course he'll see me again soon—
coffee is my weakness.
But more than coffee
he ...

By the time I return home
I've made my decision,
and it had nothing to do with Mum's encouraging.
I'll go out fishing on the boat.
If I suggested "coffee"
at Café Legato ...
I wouldn't be there
to spend time with Dad.

# Banana Bread, Please

Awoken with alarm.
*Beep*
*Beep*
*Beep*
*Beep*
It echoes
down the hallway
and into my room.
It should have woken
the whole household.
But the house is
still
    and
        silent.

I hear
a muffled
*thump.*
Dad's alarm clock finally stops.
I breathe
to slow
the pounding in my ears.

After the squeak of his bed,
I sniffle a little
in the cool morning air.

Wait for his footsteps.
Then curl back into a ball,
not ready to push back
the blanket of warmth.

'Morning, Rina.
Forecast of storms later on,
so we want to make an early start.

Rise and shine,
my petal.'

I knew it would be an early start
and hard to push up from bed.
So I slept
in my best fishing clothes:
a grandpa T-shirt
and denim shorts,
with swimmers underneath.

I roll over and out.
Slip on my deck shoes,
sling my bag over my arm,
    and shuffle out
          to the car.

'I haven't made coffee.
Didn't want to wake your mother
or the others.
We'll stop by Café Legato
for something to eat.'

The café.
His eyelashes
and smile that
crush
my heart
every
time.

Josh.
Always
and
forever.
Josh.

Dad stops the car at the curb.
'I'll give the others a quick call and
make sure they're on their way.
You go order.'

My heartbeat
          thuds
in my ears.

I pause for a moment
to watch him,
unaware
of my eyes
drinking in every detail
just one more time
before I push through the door.

'Rina, you're early,'
Josh says with a smile.

'You're making coffee,'
I say,
so we've both
stated the obvious.

'Latte?'
He blinks.
The breeze from his lashes
encourages my words
as I untie my tongue.

'And a caramel capp, raisin toast, and
gluten-free banana bread.'
I close my mouth,
saliva caught between
my tongue and throat.

I hadn't taken a breath.
I attempt to ...
swallow
breathe
cough
at the same time.

Josh just smiles
and flaps his lashes.

My face burns.

'Toasted?'
He points to the banana bread.

I nod.
Safer than talking.

Dad walks in
and saves me
from myself.

Josh pushes the drinks forward
on the counter.
'The capp's for your dad?'

We all know it is.
Dad smiles,
hands over cash.
Josh's lips part.
They always do
as he smiles.

The pull as strong as ever.
I hold the counter

knowing I'm
      leaning towards him
for the second time
this week.

Dad turns to leave.
I follow.
Josh speaks words
that meld with our footsteps.
'Maybe drop in again tomorrow
'round ten.
I'll be on a break.
Want to hang out?'

'The others are there and ready to go,'
Dad tells me.

But I'm still back at Josh
being on a break
tomorrow,
wanting to hang out.

I look from Josh to Dad.
Did I hear right?
Did Josh really say,
'Want to hang out?'
Or did I just imagine those words?

I look somewhere between
Josh and Dad,
then from one to the other,
nodding—
hoping they both
think the nod
is intended for them.

# Josh

In eighteen years
he's travelled the world.
From London to Paris
and Johannesburg to LA.

As a kid
I watched him return
after each trip
with new clothes,
new toys.

When he turned twelve
we waved him off
over the back fence.
Not sure when we'd see him again.
Not sure if we'd be friends when he returned.

His parents shipped him off
to board at a school,
while they continued
their business,
tripping around the world.

'Not good enough for us, hey?'
the locals would tease.

But he'd always keep his cool.
With a nod
he'd retreat.

As kids,
we'd yell from our backyard,
inviting him to join us.
He'd jump the
woven wire fence
in one bound.

When strong winds blew
the links rattled
warming my heart,
reminding me
he was away.

After living at school
in another city,
for five years,
he returned home
to live over our back fence.
And continue his study
via correspondence.

Now rusty and on a lean,
held up only by tangled shrubs,
the fence still separates
his home from mine.

When I hear
his stereo
thumping through the air,
it's like an alert telling me
*Josh is home.*

Every tune
Every band
Every sound
Hits my soul

It's like he reads my mind,
hears my music,
then plays it on his stereo.

'You wanna come play?'
was no longer a question.

# All Aboard

Boating terms fly,
fishing utensils clatter.
I plug in my earbuds
and turn up my music,
only enough to hear,
but not miss,
the conversation
around me.

Dad and I won't find
our quality time
on the cruise out.
I'll have to wait
until the anchor is
ditched
and when his line is in.

Johnno, Jayden,
Al and Kai
nod my existence
and continue their prep.

'Should go out more often.'
Johnno elbows Dad
as he passes him.

'I think this will be
our last
for a couple of months.'
Dad checks everything once more.
Safe and secure—
never a moment of chance.
He keeps everything safe.

Al and Johnno chuckle.
'Mumma Mia about to drop?'

Al flicks the pull ring
on the can in his hand.
His Coke fizzes,
spilling on his deck shoes
    and
        across the floor.

Dad sighs.
I know he'll be itching
to clean up after his friend.
But he doesn't.
Instead, he looks up and nods.

Was he sad?
Disappointed?

I know my dad
but I didn't know that sigh.

Mia,
my mum,
pregnant
with baby number six.

I stare at the spilt Coke
and want to mop it up
so we could start the day
fresh,
clean,
unblemished.

# Heart of Our Home

Home is where the heart
of many of us live.
Mum and Dad fell in love,
bought a house block
in a narrow street.
Their dream fulfilled
with a hill and a valley
contained within their fence line.

Mum said she loved the natural flow.
Dad said it would have cost too much to level.
And so they built a split-level house
across the valley and hill.
The land is still uneven.

The entrance ... not so grand.
Two steps up
      a porch
that leads to the
      lounge room.
Turn the corner ...
      our kitchen.
Up five more steps
      our bedrooms.
Three bedrooms
      where five kids
           drop their weary heads each night.

Outside our bedroom
      is a ladder
leading to an attic
that's not quite
on top of the house.
It's where we store stuff.
And with seven of us,
there's a lot of stuff.

Up another six stairs,
Mum and Dad built their haven—
big enough to swing an elephant.
'Our treat of a retreat,'
they've always told us.

We were all planned.
Me first,
then three years later,
Zach.
After him came the twins—
Shakiya and Matilda.
Planned,
but no one expected two at once.
Mum said she was thankful
Zach and I
were in school by then.
Once Mum and Dad got over
the double bundle,
along came Kane.

Right from the beginning
they knew they'd need
a room to get away—
from the noise,
from the craziness,
from the family.
Pretty smart of them,
I think.

But then came number six.
The only one not planned.
I overheard Mum cry.
I overheard Dad tell her
we'd be all right.

But
Mum was sad for weeks.

It was hard to watch.
I never knew the right words.
I tried to stay out of her way.

Now that her belly
is bigger than an oversized watermelon
she seems happy again.

# Home on a Boat?

'Make yourself at home,'
Dad tells me.

He pulls the ropes
from the
pontoon.

The boat drifts,
rocking,
until the motor
kicks into gear
and Dad takes the wheel,
giving us all direction.

We bounce over
    small
        ripples
            of waves.

I grip the seat.
At home
I'd never have to grip
anything
to stay
in one spot.

Kai sits beside me,
tapping his hand
on his leg
to the
*ksch*
*ksch*
*ksch*
that escapes his headphones.

I turn my music up.
Ignore the
*ksch*
*ksch*
*ksch*
and realise
I'm feeling more at home
than I would have
ever expected.

# Music Wars

Music often danced
between our rooms.

I smile
at the thought.

Zach and his heavy metal.
Shaka and Mattie with their
tweeny, boppy, bouncy tunes.
Kane with some crazy
kids' show soundtrack,
and me
in the groove with mainstream pop.

Mum and Dad
sing along
to whatever is nearest
and whichever they know the words to.
They never tell us to turn it down,
unless it's nap time
or sleep time
at night.

I turn to Kai.

'What?' He shrugs.

Yeah—
Almost just like home.

# Cruising

The motor *wrrrs* softly.
A tingle of misty spray
peppers my face.
My ponytail
stings my back
like a whip
covered with salt.

I pull my cap
tighter,
tucking my hair under
as I drain the last of my latte.

Did Josh really say those words?
Surely I wasn't dreaming.
*'Want to hang out?'*
The words
I want to say
to him—
every time
he blinks at me.
Words I've wanted to say
ever since he returned
from school
miles away.

But I've never
found the courage
to release them
from my lips.

He chose
to speak the words aloud.
Sweet.
Sensational.
*'I'll be on a break.'*

Tomorrow morning at ten,
there's nowhere else I'll be.
Café Legato
is wooing me.

Not the café,
but the boy
behind
the
counter.

I replay the moment
over and over
in my mind ...

Footsteps ...
Dad's voice ...
Josh's voice ...
The swish of the door ...
My head nodding ...
Did I even find a smile?
Or was I lost in the moment,
numbed by his words?

# Numb

Numb,
like a cold wind.

Numb,
like snow on your feet.

Numb,
like you are completely lost.

Numb,
from Josh's engaging words.

# Thawing

The slap of the water
on the side of the boat
somehow
thaws my numbness.

The sky,
clearer than crystal.
I wonder where those
forecasted storms lurk.

I close my eyes.
And feel
    my lips
        pressing
            against his.
Josh—
a welcome
invasion
to my mind.

# Skating

'Sooooo Rina,
Who you pretending to smooch?'
Jayden's silhouette
beams a smile,
flashing bracered teeth.

'Where's your skateboard?'
The first words that came to mind
                        popped out.
Because of course
he'd have his skateboard
on a fishing boat.

Not.

'Rina's crushing on someone,'
he sings at the top of his lungs.

Dad turns
in my direction.
His smile wide.

Does he even know
what crushing means?

He's probably
still stuck
back in the eighties
with
'got the hots for'.
    Which he still has
for my mum,
and tells her
often.

# Love

Dad loves Mum
Mum loves Dad

It's a canvas they had made,
with words inside a huge red heart,
and stuck it
on the wall
in our living room.

Like we'd ever forget.

They full on kiss.
Often.
In front
of us.
Making us cringe.

None of my friends'
parents kiss
like mine do.
Movie style.

And hand holding—
they do
whenever they're near
each other.

Though I cringe ...
It's a nice kind of rare,
safely surrounded
with their love.
A love
that
secures our family.

# Cabin Fever

The air is shrinking.
No way out.
Five and a half metres
from the tip
to the motor.
Choking my lungs.

I wander downstairs
to the small nook.
Fridge.
Sink.
Bench.
And a tiny bed,
fit for one—
the size of my brother, Kane,
who's five.

I open
Dad's esky,
pull out an apple,
pocket a gluten free lollipop,
and check the time.
7:20 AM.
At least another
two hours
out at sea,
in shrinking air.

# Dirty

Boy, was Kane dirty with Dad.
So angry
he threw a fist.
The punch hit Dad in the stomach,
as Kane demanded to come along.
But no.
He missed out.
I got the ride.
Yippee for me.
Super boo hoo for him.

Kai trudges down the steps,
looking greener than his
impractical skate shoes.
    Pasty.
        Ill.

'Lie there.'
I point to the tiny bed.

He pulls his knees to his chest.
Lies on his side.
'Bucket,' he whines.

Witnessing puke
is not my thing.

I bin my half-eaten apple,
find a bucket under the sink.

Just in time.

His stomach
    purges
        loudly.

Echoing off the
fibreglass
surroundings.

The stench forces me away.
I head outside
to find Al,
tell him
his boy is sick.

Al laughs.

I wonder if he took me seriously?
'Like, puking,' I tell him,
with actions.

Al laughs again.

I kick off my shoes
and make my way
to the front
of the boat.

My toes firmly link
the silver rod
keeping me on board.
I lie back
on the smooth surface.
Warm.
Calm.
Free.

The drone of the motor
lulls me away,
back
to the café.

The breeze,
like a draught
blowing from his lashes.

The warmth of the sun,
inviting,
just like his smile.

His voice lingers
in my ears,
whispering,
*'Want to hang out?'*

But too soon,
I'm interrupted again.
The motor
chokes.
Cuts.

This is the part
Kane wanted to come for.
He loves the catch.
I bet he's still brewing
at home.
I wonder how Mum is coping?

# Hook and Sinker

They drop the large hook
to hold the boat
from straying afar.

Our boat is now
a vessel that drifts
but is anchored.

Waves lap,
slapping the sides of the boat,
rocking us.

Dad pulls out his rod,
loads the sharp, fish-catching hook.
Casts it far ...
then makes himself comfy.

He knows the deal.
Yes, I'm happy to accompany him.
But don't expect me
to touch any
squiggly
wriggly
worms,
hooks,
or slippery fish!

The feast of the catch.
Yes.
The catching of the feast.
No.

Many times I've been out
on a boat with Dad.
But mostly in the shallows.

This is the first time
he's taken me to deep water.
Shark infested,
I'm sure.

In the past,
our boat conversations
were light.
Nothing deep
emerged into words.

Aware of Dad's friends.
Aware of young boys nearby.
Today will be no exception.

But nonetheless,
the sway of the boat,
the glistening water,
the gentle breeze,
and salty spray,
make it tolerable.
And so I enjoy
a quiet moment
beside Dad
as he pulls in
a flipping catch.
In
and
up.

It flops
from side
to side,
and over again,
on the floor
of the boat.

# Hunting

Dad took Zach
hunting a few
weeks back.

Taught him
about guns.

I didn't sleep
the whole weekend.

What if Zach used the gun
when Dad wasn't watching?
What if he used it to ...

'Dad,
why did you take Zach shooting?'

'It's a bloke thing, love.
The hunter-gatherer in me
loves to get out
into the
wide
and
wild
open
spaces.

'Best he knows the dangers.
When to shoot.
When not to.
How to fix the safety clasp.'

'But doesn't it
like
worry you?

He might grab the gun
when you're away.'

'I have the key, Rina.'

'Even out here?'

Dad pulled his keys from his pocket.
'Yep.
The only one is in this bundle.'

I breathe a little easier
as Dad deals
with another slippery catch.
My mind slides back to Zach
and the fact that one day
he might find reason
to use the gun in the wrong way.

# Hold On

A gust of wind,
like the backdraft of a giant's breath,
flicks my cap.
It flies upwards,
floating across the air,
then plops onto the water.

'Dad?'
My eyes open wide.
Air freezes
in my chest,
like I've been punched
in the guts.

'Hold on!'
Dad's eyes
flame.
He'd seen it too.

I hold tight with both hands.
Dad wedges his rod into the holder.

# Don't Blink

The glistening water
nudging the horizon
slips behind
a sheet of ...
        What?

How is it
that the ocean suddenly looks like a sheet
hung from the sky,
instead of a rug
rolling along the floor?

It rises.
    And rises.
        And rises.

            Then curls at the top,
              with the slightest evidence of white foam ...

No way!
A king wave
big enough
        to sink a ship.

'Dad?' I yelp.

'It'll be okay, petal.
Grab your life jacket,
just in case.
But please, baby,
hold tight.'

I reach for the pink vest
while holding on to the boat
with my other hand.

In case what?
In case we're capsized?
In case the boat tips?
In case we get thrown from the boat?

I stare into the face of the wave,
demanding answers as
a deafening silence,
then a torrential crash.

The gigantic wave
splashes,
lashing
our small boat.

The front tips.

        The back dips.

                I slip.

And try not to blink.

# The Pink Jacket

I clutch the piece of pink
as the front of the boat,
and the silver bars
I'd hooked my feet under
only moments before,
slide beneath
      the surface
            of the water
                    forever.

'Love!'
I hear Dad's voice.

'Praise the Lord!'
I scream at the sound.

'Why didn't you strap that on?'
He swims towards me.

When would I have done that?
I'd barely grabbed it
when ...
*crash ...*
that
lake of water hit.

'Dad?'

'Yes, love?'
He pulls my pink jacket
in tight
and fastens it.

'The boat?'

'I reckon it's on its way to the bottom.'

'I can't see anyone!'
Like a tourniquet on my throat,
the water
shuts off my voice.

Dad nods.
His eyes leak.
And I know
it's not from the splash
of the waves.

'Clip up the other side
of your vest
and just stay here a bit.'
Dad's eyes tell a thousand stories—
none that I've ever heard.

'Sure, like where would I go?'
I say,
as I fuss with the black clasp
on the pink vest.

Dad duck dives ...
leaving me
        alone.

# Silence and Voices

A voice calls, 'Help!'

Who is it?
'Johnno?' I call,
and spin on the spot.
'Al?'

I don't have a clue which way to look
through the choppy peaks of water.
'Johnno?
Al?
You here?'

Dad hasn't surfaced.

'Johnno!'
Fear is etched all over my voice.
'Al?'
Am I hearing things?

'Rina.'

No,
that was real.

I spin again
searching in the direction
of the voice.

'Rina, anyone else with you?'
It's Johnno ...
I think.

The voice moves closer,
though I still can't see him.

White caps
and rolling waves
grow by the minute.

'Dad just dived.
He ...
he should be back.'

Johnno comes into view,
swimming towards me.

'Johnno,'
I blink.
Swallow.
'Why hasn't Dad come back up?'

Johnno squints.
Lines on his forehead,
eyes caved in
deep.
'Have you seen or heard anyone else?'

I shake my head.
Fear pulls at my stomach,
a tingle shoots up my spine.
The only thing holding me
is the pink vest
hugging my body—
clasped
secured.

# Dive

'Johnno,
I have to go.'
The urgency didn't resound
in my words.
Actions
speak for themselves.

I unclick the left,
then the right.
Slip my arms
out of the pink vest.

'Rina, no!
Wait here.'
His voice
has the pull
of an emergency.

I ignore it,
kick my legs up
and
duck dive.

'I'll go,'
Johnno says.

Too late.
I've gone.

I pull my arms
through the salty water.
Clouds overhead
cast shadows.
My vision is short—
barely two metres.

I kick deeper.
Deeper,
until my lungs burn
and my heart implodes.
Dad?
Where are you?
Dad, you can't leave me now!

My tears meld with the ocean.
I kick,
searching for air.
Upward,
in need of sunshine.
Light.
Anything less than loss
on this sinking day.

# Return

I shoot through the surface.
A surge of water rolls,
lifting me high.
I spin,
scanning
three hundred and sixty degrees.

'Dad!
Johnno?'

The next wave
lifts me to see a flash of pink—
the piece of pink
I left behind.

'Rina,' Dad calls.

We swim.
Freestyle.
Dad drags the life jacket
until we meet
in the Pacific Ocean,
miles from shore.

I embrace him.
He pushes me back,
slips my arms through the pink vest,
fastens one clasp,
then holds me again.

In the closeness,
he shudders against my shoulder.
His tears drip onto my cheek
like warm rain.

I'm too scared to look at him.
I've never seen him cry,
until now.
And that makes it
twice in one day.

# The Swimmer

I look around.
'Johnno?'

Dad points.

And I can just make out
his arms
swinging
freestyle.

'Is he crazy
or smart?'

'Perhaps ...' Dad says.
His gaze still glued to Johnno.
'I don't know, Rina.
I don't know.'

'Why don't we swim with him?'
I begin to paddle in his direction.

'No, love.'
Dad pulls me back.
'We aren't going to swim.'

I want to fight Dad,
but the stone stare
in his eyes
tells me to calm down.

'Pray.'

He could.
I wasn't about to.

'Lord, show us land
or send someone from the land to us,'
says Dad.

I check behind and in front.
No one.
Prayer not answered.

'Love, we can't be sure
we'd head directly to land right now.
All we'd do is exhaust ourselves.
We need to save as much energy as we can.
One of them will make it back soon.
They'll send someone to save us.'

'Is it because I'm a girl?'

'No, love.'

'If it were one of the boys
You'd make a swim for it, too.
Wouldn't you?'

'No, love.
To swim
for the sake of a swim
isn't the right thing to do
right now.'

# Sleeping

'Dad,
what about Kai?'

Dad's eyebrows arch.

I continue.
'He was sick.
Sleeping.
Under.'

I spin again,
expecting Kai to materialize
and splash me in the face.
I look at Dad—
his expression hard,
like he's trying not to crumble.

'I'm sorry love.
It went down so fast.
I didn't see him.
Or Al.
Jayden ...'

Is he?
Are they?

I don't want to know.
I could imagine they swam, too.
All three of them back at shore
with Johnno.
About to send help
to Dad and me.
A chopper will come and drop a line
any minute.

We'll be fished up
out of the sea
and toasty warm at home again,
and this image
of being lost in the ocean
will become a vague memory.

# Rhythm

Each rolling wave
like a rhythm
lulling me to sleep.

Minutes surrender to hours.
My water resistant watch
still reads seven-thirty.
I estimate
the time of sinking.

That little fishing boat
now
somewhere on the bed
of the Pacific Ocean.

My mind can't comprehend
how my body rhythm
is ready for sleep.

'Rina!'

'What?' I react to the call.

'You're closing your eyes,'
Dad says,
like he's had the fright
of his life.

'It's ...'
I don't know what it is.

'Tired?'
Dad grabs the unclasped clip
of my pink jacket.

My eyes still want to droop,
close
and ignore the scene in front of me.

'You're in shock, love.'
Dad clips the other clasp together,
locking me into the
pink water frock.

I nod
and blink away the weariness.
Water for miles.
It's all I can see.

'Dad?'

'Yes, love.'

'Where's the land?'

Dad thrusts his arms and legs
until he rises
at least
half a metre
out of the water.

He spins,
points.
'That way, I think.'
He looks up
towards the sun.
'Yes, it must be that way.'

Was he trying to convince
me or himself?

# Next

'Do you know what's coming next?'
Dad asks in a ridiculously jovial voice.

'Huh?' I want to shake him. 'A wave?'
How could he speak riddles at a time like this?
For goodness sake!

He looks over his shoulder.
His face taut.
A moment goes by
before he relaxes again.

'Well, we haven't told anyone yet.
We wanted the gender of our last baby
to surprise everyone.'

'So are you going to tell me?'
Bobbing up and down
in the middle of the sea
I couldn't care less which it would be—
boy or girl,
girl or boy.
Whatever.
Just get me out of here.

Dad grins.

'It's a boy?'
Why else would he grin like that?

He shakes his head.

'A girl?' I ask,
knowing he wanted another boy
to even things out.

'A girl! You're right.
Can you believe it?'
His face glows with joy.
I wonder if he was this excited
about me when they received
the ultrasound results
before I was born.

'I'm so blessed already,
to be surrounded by so much beauty.
And now another one.
Another delightful
daughter of beauty
is about to come into this world.'

Now he was going over the top.
'Dad, are you serious?'
Delirious?

'Of course.'
His grin says he is.

'It's just ...' I stumble on my words.
'I thought ... you'd want another boy.'

'Rina.' He grabs my hand.
'If she's as lovely as you,
there's no other I'd desire.'

My heart flutters.
My eyes blur with tears.
'Thanks, Dad.'

# Babies

Each time a baby,
or babies,
arrives,
our home is turned
upside down.

We would jump like we'd had
an overnight surprise,
that we knew about
but forgot to prepare for.

I still remember
baby Zach in my arms.
His body resting in my lap,
while Mum's hand held his head.

I was at school
when the twins
tumbled
into
this world.
I begged to stay home,
but Mum and Dad insisted
I head off to school.

Kane arrived just before Christmas.
I was granted the last week off school.
Mum was sick.
It was bed rest for her.
I got to play mummy.
I loved every minute,
though it showed me
            the truth.
Being a mum could wait
                a while.

Nappies,
nappies,
nappies!

Mum insisted
cloth was better
for the environment.

Smelly.
    Leaky.
        Awkward!

'Can we please buy disposable?' I'd asked.
I was the main nappy changer.
One day, I counted fifteen.

Gah!

'Sure, love.' Mum raised her eyebrows.
'If you go out to earn some money
to cover the extra expense.'

I took that as a no.

Scrape.
    Soak.
        Wash.
            Hang.
                Fold.

I willed Mum to recover quickly.

My summer holidays were spent
washing,
cooking,
cleaning,

'til Mum was
able to
take over.

They vowed
that
was
it!

No more babies.
We were a family
large enough.

Maybe that's why she cried
when she fell pregnant again.
Maybe the memory of
illness and pain had returned.
Maybe she'd had enough.

# Relief

An increase of weight
expands inside.
I need to go ...
in an ocean ...
without toilets.

'Um, Dad?'

'Yes, love.'

'I'm busting to go,
but there's no bathroom.'

'No, there isn't one.
Not out here, anyway.'

'Do you reckon they'll find us soon?'

'Sure they will.'
He looks over his right shoulder,
and then his left.
'But just in case they're running late,
I won't tell anyone
if you go right here.'

I shouldn't have said anything.
All I'd done
was draw heat to my face.

I swish away from him a little.

'Don't go too far.'

The urgency in his voice
pulls me closer

than I'd planned to be
when I relieve myself.

I swim back.
Keep within an arm span.
To be separated by an ocean swell
might send me into a panic.
I need Dad in this moment,
just like
his urgent voice
needs me
to stay near.

I link my arm around his elbow.
Water rises and falls.
Miles and miles of water.
No land to been seen.

# Zach

If his music wasn't
            thumping
through the floor
he'd be wearing headphones,
tapping his foot.
And his brain would be
thumping
with the heavy
boom,
screech,
scratch
heavy
metal.
His music of choice.
It hurt my ears,
but for him
it somehow
soothed.

The way I see it,
he hit puberty
and freaked out.
He thinks he's in control
when he numbs his mind
by playing the loudest,
heaviest
music on earth.

Eyes always hidden
under his brunette
shards of hair.
Overdue for a haircut,
but not long enough
to look like it was meant to be
that length.

He dumped footy and cricket
a year ago.
Guitar now his focus.
Electric.
Plugged in.
Amplified.
Enough to send any parents senile.
But not ours.

'That's great!'
Dad would yell through Zach's door
when he arrived home from work.

Once,
I complained to Mum
that I couldn't concentrate on my homework.
She told me to get used to distractions—
life was full of them
                          always.

Perfect parents for a heavy metal kid.
I miss the kid
who kicked the ball
in the backyard.

# Brother

I miss
hanging out with my brother.
I hope
I can see him again soon.

'Dad?'

'Mm.'

'How have you always been
so encouraging
with Zach and his music?'

'It brings him joy.'

'I don't see much joy.'

'He's hit a hard spot.
I see him change
with music.'

'But half of it's about killing yourself.'

'Which half?'

I shrug.
I've never really been able
to work out the lyrics.
Never had a chance to read them.
It just sounds ugly to me.

Dad grins.
'Some of what he listens to
is Christian music.'

When?
Which?

'Some of that heavy stuff is actually about God.'

'No way.'

Dad chuckles.

'That doesn't make sense.'

'When he started enjoying heavy metal,
I remembered a few bands
that sing great lyrics
with a heavy sound.'

'So you gave him that music?'

'Not all of it.
He's sourced
a few himself.
Some I'd rather not hear.
But I see his face shows life,
and if it takes heavy metal
to bring him back
        out of his shell,
your mother and I say,
"Bring it on."'

I check Dad's face
to see if he's pulling my leg.
His honest eyes stare back.

I resolve to never tell Zach
to turn down his music again.

Right now,
I wish I could feel the strum of his guitar
vibrate through the floorboards
against my feet.

Something brushes
        against my toes.

I jump
   out of
      my skin.

# Danger

'Dad!'
I squeal.

'What is it?'
He grabs me close.

'Something just touched my leg.'

'Wasn't me.'

'I know that.'
Seriously!

Dad dips his eyes under water
'Fish, love.'

I let go of the breath
that had frozen in my chest.
I see them, too.
A school of fish
              swimming away.

'It was only a fish,'
he says again.

I realise my whole body
is trembling
in his arms.

# A Sound

My ears prickle.
A new sound—
not a swish or ripple,
but an echoing.

I've barely stopped shaking
from the slither
against my leg
and I'm faced with
this new sound of echoing
getting louder every second.

'Dad, you hear that?'

'I do.'

We both spin
on the spot.
Searching.
Listening.

A thump
cuts the atmosphere,
vibrates
through my skin.

'Chopper?'

'I think so.'
Dad raises one arm,
waving with vigour.

I grab the sleeve
of his other.

The sky patched
with clouds and blue.
Chopper unseen.

'If we can't see them
how will they see us?'
I don't want Dad
to waste his energy.

'It's getting louder.
Surely we'll see it soon.'

The hope in Dad's voice
pushes me
to raise my arm, too,
and wave.

I kick my legs
and stay close to Dad.
To save us.
To save him.
To save me.

The ocean
continues to roll.
The thought of
being swallowed whole,
by the swell,
into the depths below,
pushes me to wave harder.

'Rina!'
Dad points
over my head.

I look up.
I look around.
I see it.

Hovering above the ocean,
blades chopping,
waves lapping higher.
Though the chopper
is too far away
to have caused
the waves.

'Surely they'll see this.'
I kick higher
out of the water,
letting the pink vest
surge toward the sky.

Our arms flap.
Urgent.

Our attempt
to call them in,
wasted in the expansive ocean.
The water claims a win.

The chopper flies away.
We drop our arms.
Dad sinks
a little too far.
I rip him back up.

'Don't you dare
sink on me now!'

'Sorry, love.
Just relaxing
the muscles.'

'Lean on this.'
My vest,
buoyant enough to hold us both
until someone comes to our rescue.

# Alyssa

We were meant to play tennis
this afternoon.
She'll be waiting.
Wondering.
Would anyone tell her
I haven't returned?

She'd beat me anyway.

Alyssa–
always the sporty one.

I was only good at backyard cricket.
Alyssa could
   swim
      dance
         sprint
            hurdle
               golf

When it came to Alyssa
and sport,
she excelled.

Except bowling a cricket ball.

In between sport,
she swooned over boys.
        Several at once.

Never tying herself down to one.
Never giving her heart to another.
But she'd come dangerously close
                      many times.

Most call her a flirt.
To me, she exudes love.
She loves everyone.
Hate isn't a word in her world.

Wish I had my racquet with me now.
I could go straight there,
meet her,
when we get saved.

If we get saved.

# Sun

Through patches of cloud,
I watch the sun
slide
seamlessly across the sky,
dipping
towards the west.

'What time do you
reckon it is?'
I check my watch
one more time.
It still reads seven-thirty,
even though hours
      of floating
have passed.

'Maybe two o'clock,
maybe three.
This time of year,
the days begin to stretch.
It's hard to tell.'
Dad rubs his eyes.

'The chopper didn't return.'
In fact, I haven't seen anything
in the sky
since the chopper.
It's like all flying machines
have taken a holiday.
Or worse,
been grounded.

'Yeah, I noticed too.'
Dad doesn't even look up,
but instead
stares into the water.

His eyes crease
with concern.
Lines etch
into his forehead.
Is he losing hope?
Are we doomed?

I clench my teeth
and grit away
unnecessary
emotion.

Silence
and soft water music
dance around us.
The hours
move time forward,
until
the sun rolls
behind the land
we cannot see,
but know is there.

# Hungry

My stomach lurches,
echoes through the water,
sending saliva
swirling in my mouth.

Banana bread
was the last
I'd eaten,
other than that bite
of apple
before I threw it
in the bin.

'The lollipop,'
I tell Dad, and reach
into my pocket.
I find the sticky mess,
still inside the wrapper.
Cracking it with my teeth,
I offer Dad half,
then suck as much
off the paper as I can.
Dad licks his fingers.
It goes too quickly
and doesn't even nudge
                away the hunger.

My stomach lurches,
again.
Hungry.

All I want is
banana bread
from Josh.
Toasted.

# Glow

The inky blue
succumbs to
pitch black
darkness,
and we wait
in hope of
a lunar glow.

# Coeliac

'I'm hungry,'
I tell Dad.

'I packed some food.
Some of your favourites.'

'I know.'

Dad is the best at catering
for that niggling health issue I have.
Where others found toleration hard,
he found it a breeze
to ring ahead
or prepare at home
and always make sure
I'd have something to eat.

'Thanks, Dad.'

He wraps his arms
around me.

I wonder which treats
he'd packed
that had
     sunk
        to the depths
           of the ocean.
But I don't ask.
Instead, I let his arms
cradle the emptiness
inside.

Raw fish would be
our only option,

but neither of us
have the energy
to dive,
grab,
pluck
those speedy,
flipping,
slippery
creatures
from the water.

Not to mention
what we'd have to do
to actually eat them.

At least they'd be gluten free ...

I move my focus
to the stars,
beginning to twinkle,
and wonder if something greater
is actually there
and
could actually save us?

# Under the Stars

When I was eleven,
Zach nine,
Josh twelve,
we took our dinner
outside,
lay on our backs
and watched the clouds
form shapes.

Elephants.
Clowns.
Ducks.

With each new discovery,
our laughter
dimpled the air.

'Dare you to sleep out,'
Zach said.

Bellies full,
dusk falling heavy,
I was up for the challenge.

'Why not?'

Josh laughed.

Mum came out.
Josh's dad, too.
They couldn't woo us inside,
so they brought
some of the inside
                out.

They dumped picnic rugs,
sleeping bags,
mozzie repellent,
and torches
in a pile beside us,
then retreated indoors
                         laughing.

The shapes in the clouds
soon blended with the darkness
of night.
We set up our beds in a row.
Josh, Zach, then me.

And we slept.
No fear.
Just fun.

# No Return

They didn't return—
those lifeguards
in the chopper.

They didn't turn back around.
They left.
Blades thwacking.
Safety light flashing.

How could they not
look a little lower,
a little closer,
a little longer
to find us?

I clenched a fist into a ball,
thrashing it through the water.
Violence wasn't me,
but right now
I could put a hole
through something.

I could kick my way
through a wall.
Punch my arms
through the water
to find land.
I could.
I would.
I'd try,
but it's pointless
in this darkness.

# Angry

'You seem angry.'
Dad rubs my back.

'Argh!'
I punch the water.

'They'll come back, love.
Remember to have faith.'

Here comes
that mustard seed again.
He never lets up;
never lets it go
or leaves it at home.

Dad and his mustard seed
go everywhere.
If anything ever goes wrong,
all he ever says is,
'Just the size of a mustard seed.
Never lose faith.'

Now accustomed to the darkness,
I look into his tranquil eyes.
They relax something deep within me
and force me to calm down.

His demeanour of peace
let me
let go.

# Bedtime Stories

Dad stretches an arm
out of the water.
The darkness
        hovers
as finally the awaited moonlight
casts its shadows.

His arm strong.
His hand tender,
        loving.

He strokes
my saltwater-crusted hair
and hums.

As I cling to my father,
drifting in the ocean,
I'm taken back to my bedroom ...
years before.

'Again, Mum.
Again,' I'd cry.

Each night, the same book.
*Time for Bed* by Mem Fox
captivated me.

She'd always give in
and read it again,
but she'd stop after
three times through.
With kisses and cuddles,
she'd tuck the sheet in tightly
and call out to Dad.

I'd wait for the stairs to creak,
and the scuffs of his feet,
and anticipate the fun
he was about to bring.

He'd bounce on the bed,
loosening the sheets,
then he'd tickle
and poke me 'til
I couldn't breathe
a breath.

But he'd keep the best 'til last.
I'd wait enthusiastically
for the song that he'd sing.
A song he wrote
my first day
here on earth.

> *Valerina,*
> *Valerina,*
> *sweeter than*
> *a ballerina.*
> *Lovely child,*
> *born today,*
> *could there be*
> *any as sweet as she?*
>
> *Valerina,*
> *I'll call*
> *her Rina.*
> *She'll be strong.*
> *She'll be courageous.*
> *Protected always by me.*

*Valerina,*
*my dear Rina.*
*I'll always*
*remember how*
*she stole my heart*
*that very first day.*

Almost as if
he reads my thoughts,
Dad hums the tune.

I hear his words
clear in my mind.
I hum along
with him.

# Red

Al was wearing red,
and he was as round
as a blimp.

Could he have?
Would he have
made a swim for it?

Would Al and Johnno
be together now,
telling the coastguard
where we were?
Showing them on the map
where the boat went down?

We could have
    drifted
        miles
            by now.

The waves peak higher.
White caps shine
under the moon.

I hope Al and Johnno have made it.
I hope one of them has rung Mum.
I hope they send
someone to our rescue.

Is hope the same as faith?
Is my hope even close
to the size
of Dad's mustard seed?

# Droop

I feel my eyes
droop
heavily
as Dad pulls me close.

Though strong,
he's slight and, perhaps,
our saving grace
is in our size—
held up by the piece of pink
for one,
but holding the two of us
in the black peaks
of white-capped water.

# Snap

My eyes snap open.
The glow makes me blink.
The moon already
a quarter
through its walk
for the night.

'Glad you're awake again, my girl.'
Dad's teeth glisten
as he smiles.
'Don't know how much longer
I could have held your chin high.'

I don't know if I feel rested
or worse for the nap,
but how can I thank Dad
for his fearless
wakefulness,
strength,
and support?

'Ahh!' I scream,
wrap my
legs around him.

'What is it?'

'Something just
touched me.'

'It'd be a fish.
Like earlier on.'

'What if it's a ...'
The word catches on my tonsils.
'Shark?'

'In the name of Jesus!' Dad shouts.
'Protect us from all dangers.
Surround us with your angels
until we're safely rescued.'

Great time to play
the Jesus card, Dad.
'Like he can help us.'

'Faith, love.
Faith the size of a mustard seed.
That's all you need.'

I have faith in Dad.
He'd never let anything
happen to me.

I have faith in the pink vest.
It has held both of us up
until this point.

But faith in a Jesus?
Faith that a God could stop a shark?
Or keep us from drowning?
I'm not sold on that.

# Prayer

Dad continued ...
'You have never forsaken us,
and for that we are thankful.
Lord give us
strength
and endurance,
and thank you for your
supernatural intervention.
Please send
the chopper out again.
Please send someone
to find us.
In Jesus' name,
Amen.'

# Ink

A sea of inky liquid
drips
from my hand.
It creases,
folds,
tumbles,
and rolls.

A fresh splash
awakens.

The ink on Dad's arm
glistens
under the moonlight.
A cross
on a mountain,
faded with years
but forever marked.

'Inked,' as my best friend says.

Like Alyssa would like to be.

'Everyone's doing it,'
she often says.

Toby and Reef
already have.
But not Josh.
Well ...
not that I know of.

I'm undecided,
to ink
or not to ink—

a permanent mark,
a pretty picture
for today ...
to fade in time.

I reach to touch the cross
and wonder about his faith.

A stance I don't quite get—
a peace without control,
a power he relies on,
stronger than the bicep
on which it's drawn.

Another splash
hits my face.
Looking up, I see folds
of inky ocean,
capped with
white bubbles.

Dad's told me a thousand times,
if he knew then
what he knows now,
he would never have got it.

I don't understand completely,
but he's read words from the Bible,
his reasoning for never going back for more.

And as I look from his arm
back to the inky water,
I decide
inking isn't for me.

# Flash

Our glowing moon
fights with
puffs of cloud
until
it fades beneath,
leaving darkness
in its wake.

Movement in the sky.
Light interrupts the darkness.
Irregular,
spasmodic
shards of light.
A flash.
A flicker.
A shiver
rakes my spine.

Calmness
blown away.

I tuck my crunchy hair
behind my ears,
but unbound,
it flaps
in my face,
in my eyes,
everywhere.

Soon a rumble
follows each flash.
Fierce and moving fast,
the streaks through the sky
light the path
for rain
to follow.

# To the Park

The park down the road
and around the corner
was the best
for a game of cricket.

'Let's go,' Zach said,
as he grabbed the gear,
his words more an order
than a suggestion.

I followed him out,
swinging my arm to warm up.
My speedy bowl
always got him out.

A tinkle,
rattle,
rattle,
followed by footsteps
from over the back fence.

He was coming.
My friend,
Zach's mate.
Back this week
for us to enjoy.

Though the other kids laughed,
Zach didn't.
He let Josh join in.

I never bowled Josh out.
The only one I couldn't get.
Before we started,
I knew he'd outsmart me
again.

Up and down the street,
the word spread fast.
All the kids we knew
met us at the park.

Sweltering under the sun,
the creek would have been smarter.
But Zach had the bug.
He needed to play cricket,
and we all chose to comply.

Even at ten,
Zach was often
    low,
          sad,
                down.

Even back then,
when he was in a mood
and wanted to do something,
we'd give in,
let him have his way—
anything else
wasn't worth the pain.
If it was cricket he wanted,
          a game was on.

I hated seeing him lose it.
I prefer to play his way,
keep him happy—
rather than get my way.

Zach raced ahead.
I slowed my pace
as Josh caught up.

# Conversation

He told me about
his flight home the night before,
and how the flight attendant
dropped dinner
all over his lap.

He laughed.

I laughed.

I loved when Josh
returned home
and reminded me
how much I missed
him being round.

# The Game

Twelve of us
stood in a huddle,
six a side.
Easy as,
with even numbers.

One team
shirts,
the other
shirts off.

Girls automatically
in the shirts on team—
of course.

Zach pulled his shirt off,
announced he was captain,
and Josh could head up the other team—
        shirt on,
        with me.

A twenty-cent coin
thrown in the air.
The toss decided
shirts off to bat first.

Zach was first up.
I swung my arm,
grabbed the taped tennis ball
and stalked back
past the stump
we used as the wicket.

My first bowl
ordinary,
off target and wide.

Zach cut the ball
                    to the boundary
for four.

Everyone laughed.

Had they forgotten
it was usually me
who got them out?

I jogged back to my mark,
focused on middle stump
painted on the tree trunk,
and sped in once again.

Zach made contact.
The ball shot up
into the air.
Josh and I both ran.
He called, 'Mine!'
I let him go for it.

Bowled me.
Caught Josh.
We made a great team.

Zach slammed the bat on the ground.
'No ball!' he yelled,
but hung his head
and passed the bat
to the next guy in.

Both teams,
red faced and sweaty,
enjoyed the shade
as dark clouds gave reprieve
from the stifling heat.

When lightning flashed,
kids started to leave.
Chased home
by claps of thunder.

Zach's eyes wide
and wild.
'Dare you not to leave.'

'Don't be a git.
It's looking green.'
Josh stared off
towards the west.

A flash blinded me.
      I jumped.
Deafened by thunder
a second after.

Stones of ice
sliced through the air,
leaving gashes on my arms
'til I found shelter
under a picnic table.

Josh grabbed Zach,
but Zach stood firm.
Hail bruising them,
cutting their skin
'til they were streaked with blood.

The hail grew larger.
A horn blasted.
'Get in, you idiots!'
Dad slid open the van door.

Josh dragged Zach.
I clenched my fists,
    my teeth,
        and ran.

The door rolled shut.

'You in a daring mood again, Zach?'
Dad knew.

Zach shrugged.

Josh shook flecks of ice
from his hair.

I said nothing.

# Dare You

'You know, if Zach was here,
he'd dare us not to leave.'

'I know.'

'You reckon
there's any
hail up there?'
I tip my nose
towards the clouds.

'We'll have to wait
and see.'

'I wish I could be brave …
like Zach.'

Dad pulls me close.
We grip tightly
to each other.
Above us,
the first rain
begins to fall.

'What happens when
lightning hits
the water?'
I shudder
at the
verbalised thought.
Hold my breath,
expecting the worst.

'If it's close,
I guess
we get electrocuted.'

'That's what I thought.'

'So, I've been praying
no strikes hit nearby.
Lord, keep them miles away.'

'Miles away will mean
we're okay?'

Another streak
lit the sky
and illuminated
Dad's nodding profile.

'Can you add to that prayer
for no hail to come tonight?
That stuff really hurts
when it hits in a storm.'

'For sure, love. You'd know.'
He rubs the back of my neck.

My shoulders want to release
all that is tense
under the pink vest.

The crease between his eyes deepens.
I hold my breath
for an eternity,
brace for the worst.

# Strength

It's not that I wish Zach were here.
It's just that I know he'd handle this
*way* better than me.

In his lack,
he can be
amazingly strong.

I must remember
to tell him
when we arrive home.

# A Melody

A melody plays in my mind.
A song I know.
A song I love.
It's not that new,
but I could listen to it
over
and
over.

I can hear Katy Perry's voice,
just the way I heard it
yesterday—
the last time I heard music.
One of her songs,
streaming through
the mesh fence from Josh's house
and into our backyard.

I would sing it right now,
at the top of my lungs,
if only it could connect
me with him.

Will I make it back for the date?

Will we make it back alive?

# Don't Speak

Waves crash over us
like fire-smothering blankets.
I spit out water and gasp for air.
Wind thrashes and swirls
until it pushes us further
                                out
                                                to sea.

We don't speak
through the deluge,
through the crashing thunder,
through the nightmare of the moment.

I hold tight to Dad's shirt
in case I lose grip of his hand.
Dad holds tight to my vest.

My mind screams,
wishing for a miracle,
wishing to be out of here,
wishing to be in my bed at home.

I hold onto Dad
tighter than he holds onto me,
tighter than I've held before,
tighter than I'll ever hold again.

# Calming

The rain finally dissipates,
and the gale force winds
blow the storm to bombard the ocean
further east.

Slowly,
    the air
        stills
    until it's
        quiet.

The ocean,
once again, dark
without white caps.
Almost without waves.
Calm.

We watch the light show
              slink away,
until a slight glow
shines through.

# Beside Herself

'Dad?'

'Hm.'

'Mum will be beside herself.'

'I know.'

'Isn't there something we can do?'

'Other than not drown and pray?'

'Um, yes.'

'That storm has pushed us
        further out,
               I'm sure.'
He does a three-sixty degree turn.

'But couldn't we swim back in,
bit by bit?'

'I don't know
if we'd be swimming
in the right direction.'

'That way.'
I point.
'It has to be.
The sun is coming up
over there.'

I try to make out his expression
but it's still too dark to comprehend.
'They won't find us here.'

'We can continue to pray.'
Dad began, 'Father God ...'

I switch off,
and everything in me
wishes Mum to be okay.

I imagine her sitting
in her favourite armchair,
swollen ankles resting
on the footstool.
The kids all asleep
and she's peaceful ...
then I blink
and see her pacing the hallway,
boiling the jug over and over,
losing her train of thought
then falling to her knees
until
the kids wake up.

She'd be praying, too.
I squint
in the slight morning light
and see Dad looking up.
Peace is written on his face
as he whispers,
'Thank you, Lord.'

# No Caps

No spray from white caps.
No surging waves.
Miles and miles.
No land in sight.

No roosters crowing.
No siblings racing.
No kettle to whistle.
Just the silence
and light
of dawn.

# Twenty-four Hours

The sun
now well and truly with us,
but land
makes no appearance.

'What did you have
planned for today, love?'

*Josh.*

I look away.
Do I want to go there
with Dad?

No.

'You know,
stuff.'

The date that was
meant to be today.

'Stuff like
with the girls,
or the local café,
or something else?'
Dad's eyebrows arch.

Seriously,
did he know?

'Yeah, maybe the local.'

'Ah, Cafe Legato—
just what I thought.'

'To feed my
coffee addiction.'
And to see
that beautiful face.

'You ready to talk
about him yet?'

'Who?'

'Josh. Who else?
You trying to hide
something else
from me?'

'I obviously don't hide
anything from you.'

He presses his finger
on my wrist.
'Finger on the pulse, Rina.'
He nods.
'So tell me about Josh.'

'You know him.
Not much to tell.'

'Careful.'

Like if there was something
going on
I'd have something
to be careful about.

But the guy who makes great coffee,
and smiles
with the most beautiful
eyes in the world,
has always,
only ever,
been a friend.

'Has he asked you out?'

I replay
those words
in my mind.

*I'll be on break.*
*Can we hang out?*

He did ask me out.
It really had happened.

'Funny you should ask.'

# Date

'So have you been on a date
without our consent?'
Dad's face changes in the moment.
His mouth curls down,
his eyes droop,
he turns away.

If my friends heard this conversation
they'd laugh like there was no tomorrow.
Except for Alyssa.
She knows the deal in my family.
Hers is similar.
Mum and Dad insist on giving their consent.

Always have.

Always will.

'Dad.'
I blink.
Josh's face appears in my mind.
'Yesterday—
he asked me to meet him
today.
Casual.
Not like a real date.
You know we've been friends
forever.'

It's only me who's let
my imagination
         run
                wild.

'He'd be keen.
Look at you.

Even sunburnt
and waterlogged,
you look like a princess.'

'Yeah, good one, Dad.
I was trying not to think
of what I looked like right now.'

'Nothing a little aloe
can't fix.'

# Vera

'Aloe?
Since when are you
into aloe?'

'Just something
your Mum would say.'
His eyes swell with tears.

'What if they don't find us, Dad?'

'Don't go there, love.
Faith the size of a mustard seed.'

I hold onto Dad
and dream about aloe vera,
while he
holds onto
his mustard seed faith
in God.

# Burnt

The last time
my skin singed like this,
I was with Alyssa
and her family
at the beach
for a day.

They're the olive,
always outside
family.

We're the kinda tanned
but naturally fair
family.

I acted like her for a day.
At thirteen,
I didn't want to be different.
Just wanted to blend in
and not make a fuss.

She tanned.

I blistered.

She looked gorgeous.

I spent weeks with
patchy,
peeling off skin.

Since that day,
I've plastered on
the sunscreen,
and sometimes zinc,

and sat in the shade
to avoid
the pain.

But this is worse
than that day.

Far worse.

# Blistered

Blisters
on my shoulders,
my arms,
my hands.
I fear seeing
a reflection of my face.

My lips burn with each word,
my tongue can barely move.
I blink.
Ouch!
If I blink one more time
I'm sure
my eyes will be erased
by the salt wedged
inside my eyelids.

As my eyes insist
on blinking
once more,
I let my eyelids relax
       down,
              closed.
I can't bear the pain
to open them again.

I dare not think about my feet.
They've been submerged
for longer than
I can remember.

The sun continues to dry
my lips,
my eyes,
my nose,
my cheeks.

My lips—
no longer recognised
by my tongue.
More pus-infested lumps
appear
in my mouth,
on my face
in the moment that I've lost.

I don't remember opening
my eyes again
but ...
I see Dad.
I see sun.
I see swell,
and then still water.
But my mind isn't with
the swell,
or the sun,
or my dad.

My mind is on
*Can we hang out?*

Sorry I'm late,
Josh.

# Thoughts

I think
I'm making sense
when my words begin
to jumble.

Dad is silent …
I can't remember
his last words.

The urge to speak
keeps my mouth moving.

'Shaka and Mattie,
still in their
own
world.
No room for others.
You think they'll ever have
friends other than themselves?
Or will they be like that
forever?
I miss them tagging along,
asking to tag along,
insisting on tagging me.
It's not like they talk to me
when they follow.
They prattle on to each other,
like white noise
by my side.
A hum I'd love to hear
right now.'

I will their footsteps
to come running up the stairs.

Only
    there's
        no
            stairs.

The only time they
knock back tagging along
is when I mention coffee.
They screw up their noses.
'Puewie,' they scream
and run back into their room.

I turn to Dad.
He stares into the distance.
He hasn't heard a thing.

I realise
the words have moved
to my mind.

My mouth too blistered
to speak.
My eyes too blurry
to see land,
even if it was near.

I wonder how Dad's
mustard seed is going.

# Fish

Brim
Trout
Marlin
Flathead
Barramundi
jump out of the water
around us,
circling us
like we're their game.

They jump
higher,
faster.
One flips,
the others copy.

They make me dizzy
but I can't turn away.

I spin
as they circle
and begin to dance
in
    and
        out.

Then with a partner,
they spin around each other.

If only I could catch this on film.

'Dad!' I will my mouth to move.

He clings to my vest—
no limbs move,
no light in his eyes.

The fish disappear.
The sun is high.

My eyelids darken my world.

# Blue

Blue is all I see.
Blurry blue water.
Blurry blue sky.
Water.
Sky.
Water.
Sky.
No clouds.
No choppers.
No boats.
No land.
Water.
Sky.
Water.
Sky.
Water.
Sky.

In my mind
I begin to die.

# Drift

I float ...

    drifting

        away

    somewhere.

I don't know.

# Follow

A small mustard seed
grabs my attention,
urging me to follow,
urging me to believe.

My legs take me,
but it's my heart,
overriding my thoughts,
that follows.

It floats,
a breath's distance,
ahead.

Up a steep mountain,
I lose my footing,
scrape my knees.
But the seed waits—
drawing me in,
drawing me closer.
Urging me to keep
following.

I dust off my knees
and follow,
slower this time.
The peak of the mountain
just ahead.

Three
    more
        steps
            and I'm there.

The seed rests
on a rock.

I sit beside,
and the view
is unbelievable.
I see the whole
world—
not like from space,
but right here.
It's real
and magnificent.

The seed moves again,
urging me to follow
down the mountain.

We race at crazy speed.
I tumble
      and roll
past the seed,
but it catches me
as I crash against a tree.
Ouch!

I want to stop.
I'm exhausted.
I'm hurt.
I'm in pain.
But the seed
pulls me forward
into the gully.

It's dark
and musty
with mildew,
and I need to get out.

The seed comes close.
I feel warm,
like the seed is hugging me,
and with that gentle sensation,
we move together—
slowly at first,
until momentum builds.
Before I realise it,
we are running out
of that valley
and back up
another mountain.

The seed leaves me
and leads me.

The distance
        between us
                grows fast.

# The Seed

I finally catch up
to the racing seed.
It lands
beside Dad.

When did he turn up?

He's digging a hole,
and before I know it,
he plants the minuscule seed ...

The one I've been following.
The one that urged me to keep going.
The one that hugged me when I was down.

Dad covers it with dirt,
and waters it
every day.

The sun goes up,
the sun goes down,
over and over.

I see him at the garden
tending to the seed.
It sprouts.

It grows quickly,
drawing me towards it
all over again,
making me want
to nurture it, too.

Now I'm at the garden
each day with Dad.

We weed and water
together.

The trunk thickens,
the branches spread wide,
the tree stretches high,
until its taller than Dad.

Low branches
sway in the breeze,
lifting me up
off the ground.

I look down
at Dad,
being lifted up by
another branch
and something else—
something shiny.
I can't quite make it out.

The breeze gets stronger,
whipping my hair like
there's a cyclone.
It's too early
in the season
for such a storm.

I'm falling.
The wind
        too strong.
I can't balance
on the branch
any longer.

I reach,
I grab,
I cling,
I fall
    onto something flat,
           where I let my head
                    relax.

A distinctive scent
fills my nostrils.
A distinctive taste
hits my tongue.

Mustard.

And I know
    I've now seen
        a mustard seed grow.

# Rolling Waves

I relax in the sensation of
floating
on the surges of waves
rolling underneath.

But my head
is softly resting
and my body
            horizontal.

Echoes of metal
clang.
Sweet aroma
signals saliva to gush
into my mouth.

But it stings.
My tongue
awkward,
lost
in the pit of lumps.

I urge my eyes to open,
but they press closed
like balloons are tied
over the top of them.

I move to my side
but wish I hadn't.

A groan
  escapes
    my throat.

        Footsteps.

'Just relax,'
 a voice soothes.

I let go
        again.
                Comfort.

# Awakened

Bright light
in my eyes—
first my right,
then my left.

I blink it away
to focus on the ceiling,
curtained walls,
people.

'Valerina,' a sweet
silvery voice coos.
'It's good to have you
back with us.'

I open my mouth,
but my throat
scratches,
too dry to speak.

'Here, take a sip
of water.'

I do.
Though I thought
I'd never
want to see water
ever
again.

'I'll get your mum.'
The nurse
with the silvery voice
scuffs away.

Dad!
Where is he?

Johnno,
Jayden,
Al,
Kai.
Did any of them make it?

Kai—sick in the cabin.

Tears swell in my eyes,
stinging the corners.

# Reunited

Mum's rounded tummy
appears before her face does.
I haven't seen
her move
so fast in months.

'Rina, Rina!'
Her soft hands rest
ever so gently
on my arms
as she leans in to kiss
the top of my head.
'Praise God,
my beautiful Rina is alive.'

'Dad?'
I scratch out a sound.
Hope they can understand.
I need to know.

'He's in an
induced coma.'

I close my eyes again.
I don't want to ask,
but do ...
'Will he ...?'

'He'll be fine, love.
He just needs
a little more ...
forced rest.'

I feel myself
    drift away again.

The rocking of the ocean
cooing me to sleep.

I force my eyes open,
just for a peep,
to check ...

No.
No ocean.

# Josh?

'Valerina ...'

Josh?

My full name is like a song
when spoken by his voice.
He could call me by my full name
every day of the week.

I want to roll over.
Every part of me hurts.
I force my body
to stay still
and hope the pain
stops.

Josh?
My eyelids heavy.
I want to open them,
but they stay closed.

Josh?

Voices.
Shoes shuffling.
His voice.

I'd know it anywhere.
Even underwater.

His voice
fills the room,
my head,
my heart ...

'Just let her know I'm sorry.'

Josh.

What is he sorry about?
Me?
Him?
He didn't want to see me like this?
I didn't want him to see me like this.

Silence.

Has he gone already?
My heart tears in two.
Stupid crush.

# Unknown

Al.
Johnny.
Kai.
Jayden.

Their names
fly in and out
of my thoughts.
Swirling around my mind.
Fractured.
Disguised.
Unknown.

    Needing to be known.

# Let's Play

I open my eyes—
the room is bare.

The button to buzz the nurse
rests under my arm.
But the question I want to ask
isn't something
I want to ask a nurse.
It's not a question for
      just
              anyone.

Mum,
where are you?
Dad,
are you awake yet?

Zach pokes his head
around the curtain.

'Hey.'
My face hurts
when I attempt a smile.

'You survived.'
His eyebrows rise
as he grabs a chair,
sits beside.

'I missed you.'
I want to grab his hand,
but I know he'd pull away.

'Yeah.
Right.'

'Serious.'
My mouth,
face,
throat
hurt
but I continue.
'We should have a game of cricket.'

'Haven't played in a while.'

''Bout time we ...'
I pause,
try to swallow
then continue,
'... did, I reckon.'

'You're on.
Soon as you get out of here.'

The smile forces my burnt cheeks
to crumple.
I don't care.
Under that shaggy haired,
dark cover shading,
there's a slice
of who he used to be
and who he could be again.
It shines through,
like it's breaking
his depressive interlude.

# Discovery

'Is Mum around?'

'Yeah, she's with Dad.'
Zach scratches the back of his head.
Pushes his hair down flat.

'Is he awake?'

'Yep, came to a while ago.
You've been sleeping.'
He scratches the back of his head,
again,
like he doesn't know what else to do
with his hands.

I push the button,
call the nurse.
Dad would have been brave enough
to find out.
I need to know.
*Now.*
And I don't want Zach
to be the messenger.

'I need to see Dad.'

'I thought you might.
I'll grab you a wheelchair.'
She bustles back in
before I suggest I could walk.

Zach and the nurse
help me from the bed.
I put one leg to the floor
and it feels like jelly.

The wheelchair hits
a whole new set of nerves,
but the need to see Dad
dulls the pain.

We roll into his room.
He looks worse than I feel.
His eyes blink tears
when he sees me.

Now, I've lost count
of how many times
I've seen him cry.

I can't stop my mouth
before the names spill out.

'Al?
Johnno?
Kai?
Jayden?'

'Johnno was found first.'
Dad's words rasp.

Mum rubs her round tummy,
her other hand reaches out to Dad.
'He was clinging to a buoy
less than a kilometre off the beach.'

'But the others ...' Dad's voice gravelly.
He closes his mouth.

'No one knows, love.'
Mum reaches out and strokes my hair
like she used to do when I was five.

I thought I'd cried
all the tears I needed to cry,
until this news
．．．．．．．opens the floodgates.

# Recovered

A month later,
Dad is able to
rush Mum to the hospital.

I'm in charge of the house
until she brings home the baby.
A sweet baby girl,
already named Hope
before she was born.

Mum clung to her
in her womb,
as she clung to a hope
that Dad and I would be found alive,
and that's when the baby was named.

Zach's music is playing
but not at deafening volume.
I'm listening to the lyrics
as I finish the list of chores,
and I notice
the words aren't of death and darkness
but about God and light.
I hum along while I
fold, sweep, and dust,
and allow that seed of faith
to dwell and grow
within me.

# Just a Dream

My mind returns to the hospital
and the week I spent there
before I was sent home
to finish the recovery.

I was sure it had been Josh's voice,
but I must have been mistaken.
No one mentioned his apology,
and every time I go to ask
my heart cracks into pieces
all over again.

It must have been a dream,
and simply the thought
somehow soothes my heart.

I visit the coffee shop,
hoping to catch a glimpse of *him*,
but all is lost,
in vain.

Silence
       drifts
              over the back fence.
Day after day.

Dreams of a date
now washed away.
Capsized liked the fishing boat
and lying at the bottom of my heart ...
just as the boat lies deserted
on the bottom of the ocean.

# Mess

The twins got bored
following me 'round while I cleaned.
They've been quiet
for too long.

'Shaka, Mattie,' I call.

Silence replies.

Their bedroom door
swings shut
as I climb the stairs.

'Girls?'

The mix of scents
makes me sneeze.
Lavender.
Vanilla.
Rose.
Bergamot.

I push open the door.
'Girls!
What. Are. You. Doing!?'

They look up,
guilt claims their eyes.

'We were just making perfume—' says Shaka.
'and the jar fell—' says Mattie.
'over and the colour—' says Shaka.
'went everywhere—' says Mattie
'but it'll come out—' says Shaka.
'won't it?' asks Mattie.

The doorbell rings,
saves the girls from the lashing
about to spill from my lips.

Kane's five-year-old giggle
runs up the stairs
along with the slam of
the front door.

# Heard

'Hey.' He smiles
and blinks those lashes
that send a breeze
right through me.
'Trouble with the twins?'

How much did he hear?
Was I that loud?
Did the whole street hear me scream?

I touch my face.
It blistered and peeled
and hasn't really recovered.
Still too raw
for makeup.
I threw my hair in a knob
when I woke up
and haven't thought about it since.
I fear it looks more like a nest
than a style.

My tongue is lost in my mouth.
Words I want to speak
like ...
*Where have you been?*
*Why are you here?*
*Why didn't you just jump the fence?*
all get stuck in saliva.

Kane tugs on my hand,
pulling me back to reality.

'Essential oils and dye
in the carpet.
Got any solution
how to clean it up?

The twins were making perfume
Now it's everywhere ...'
Why did my mouth run away again?
Why was I bothering Josh with this?

He hands me a latte.
I draw it to my lips
to smother any more words
that want to escape.

# A New Invitation

'You're looking better
than when I saw you in the hospital.'
His chin dips.
His lashes send another breeze.

My cheeks heat up.
He *was* there at the hospital.
It wasn't just a dream.
My heart thumps.

Kane returns
with a football under his arm.
'Come for a kick.'

My shoulders tense.
Where was he for the past month?

'Sure thing.'
Josh ruffles Kane's hair.
'Meet you out back in a sec.'

Kane runs through the back door.

Josh steps closer.
I feel his breath
and take a sip of coffee.
I welcome the bitter warmth.

'We missed our date,'
he says
with one side of his mouth up,
making half a smile.

'I was kind of
unable to get there.'

An edgy tone in my voice
cuts the air,
but Josh's expression stays the same.

'I've already forgiven you.'
He blinks another breeze
and looks at his feet.
'How about tomorrow?'

I nod.
*But can I forgive you*
*for being absent*
*this past month?*

'I'm on break at eleven,
I'll come round and pick you up.'

'Okay.'
I need to get some words
out of my mind and into my voice,
but maybe it can wait
'til tomorrow,
when Shaka, Mattie and Kane
aren't listening.

We smile like awkward twelve-year-olds.
I blink,
glance behind to see my sisters
dart around the corner,
then notice Josh
follow Kane
to kick the ball.

# Absent

I wish I'd questioned where
he'd been for the past month.

I wish I'd questioned why
he was absent during my recovery.

I wish I'd questioned him ...
but I didn't.

And so I drift
back upstairs
to tackle the mess.

# Sweetest Coffee

Josh pulls up just after eleven
in a car I didn't know he owned,
in clothes I've never seen him wear,
with a familiar smile.

'What do you think?'
He opens the car door.

I slide into the seat
and drink in
the sweet scent of coffee
that fills the air.

'Of the car
or the coffee?'

'Ha.
I know what you think of coffee.
The car ...
I bought it when I was away,
while you were recovering.
I was in Brisbane for a few weeks.'

'Oh.' I smile
and again register his absence,
let my mind sit
in the wonder of why
and all those words I haven't yet spoken.

'Did you get the message when I left?'

I shake my head.

'I knew I should have written you a note.
I should have called.'

He hangs his head,
the side of his cheek twitches
as he clenches his jaw.

'It's okay,'
I squeak.
Happy in the present moment
with the thought of his intention,
and the coffee,
and the fact I'm sitting right beside him.

Josh.
My always and forever
Josh.

# Park

He drives us
to a park,
rushes to open my door,
then grabs a rug and basket
from the boot.

We find a shady spot
overlooking the town,
and I swear my thudding heart
is about to jump
right out of my mouth.

He passes me cake.
I go to say, no thanks,
but he cuts me off.

'Gluten free.
You're coeliac right?'

I nod.
Take a bite.
Smile at his precise consideration.

'How did you do it?'
he asks.

'It?'

'You and your dad.
You were out there
for over twenty-four hours.'

The memory was still
too close.
The pain came back
with the thought.

'It's okay if you don't want to talk about it.'

'I never want to live through that again.
It was Dad.
And his faith.
He has a thing about having faith
the size of a mustard seed.
He never gave up.
Never lost hope,
and prayed
so much
it felt like
too much.
But maybe
if he didn't pray so much
we wouldn't be here today.
I think I get his faith now.
I had a weird dream ...'

Again my mouth ran away.
I'd blurted too much already.
Too many senseless words.
I drain the last of my coffee
to silence my mouth.

'I just thank God
those prayers were answered.'
Josh covers my hand with his.
'Your dad wasn't the only one praying.'

I nearly choke.
'You mean you believe too?'

'Yes.'

'Why didn't I know that?'

'You've never asked.
Plus, I cop enough from the locals
for being me.
Being a Christian as well ....'

I laugh.

He grabs my hand,
leans closer
and blinks another breeze.

'You make studying from home worthwhile.
You make brewing coffee more interesting.
You have brightened my days
and captured my heart.
Valerina,
I never
want to let you
out of my sight
ever again.'

My heart thumps.
The sweetest words
I've ever heard.
I have no words to reply.
I lean close to Josh
as his mouth parts,
like it always does,
inviting a kiss.
I accept,
and know
I never want to live a day
without
Josh.

# Mustard Seed Faith

[Jesus] replied …
'Truly I tell you,
if you have faith as small
as a mustard seed,
you can say to this mountain,
"Move from here to there,"
and it will move.
Nothing will be impossible
for you.'

Matthew 17:20

# From Michelle

Dear Reader,

In the ocean of life's unanswered questions and confusion, many people will share their opinion, but very few of those words of advice will be graced with wisdom.

Seek out wise counsel that matches with the Holy Bible. It is these words of wisdom that will keep your life abundant and on a pathway to true joy.

Life filled with
questions unanswered,
confusion and mayhem.
Voices willing to share
empty, unwise advice.

Leave unwise behind,
seek out the astute,
take counsel
in line with the
Holy Bible of truth.

Purposefully follow
these words of wisdom
to light your path
with healthy patterns—
an abundant journey fulfilled.

Love, hope, and happiness,

Michelle

# About the Author

After growing up on a dairy farm near a small country town, Michelle relocated and met the man of her dreams living by the sea. The sand and surf captured her heart, so she put down roots, started a family, and now calls the Gold Coast hinterland of Australia her home.

From farm to coast, Michelle has always enjoyed creating stories through prose and verse. She believes that healing and hope can be found through reading stories.

Her passion is to support people on life's journey—through the highs and lows—and to help them find health and fulfillment.

Michelle Dennis Evans writes page-turning stories that linger in your mind long after you read the final word.